|  |  | In the book page no. | On the CD |
|---|---|---|---|
| Come On Eileen | Dexy's Midnight Runners | 2 | Track 1 |
| Dancing Queen | Abba | 8 | Track 2 |
| Groove Is In The Heart | Deee-Lite | 14 | Track 3 |
| Holiday | Madonna | 22 | Track 4 |
| Hi Ho SIlver Lining | Jeff Beck | 40 | Track 7 |
| House Of Fun | Madness | 30 | Track 5 |
| The Loco-motion | Little Eva | 36 | Track 6 |
| Love Shack | The B-52's | 43 | Track 8 |
| Stayin' Alive | The Bee Gees | 60 | Track 10 |
| Walking On Sunshine | Katrina And The Waves | 52 | Track 9 |

**International MUSIC Publications**

Series Editor: Anna Joyce
Production Editor: Chris Harvey

Editorial, production and recording: Artemis Music Limited
Design and Production: Space DPS Limited

Published 2002

RESPECT THE VALUE OF MUSIC

# Come On Eileen

Words and Music by Kevin Rowland,
James Paterson and Kevin Adams

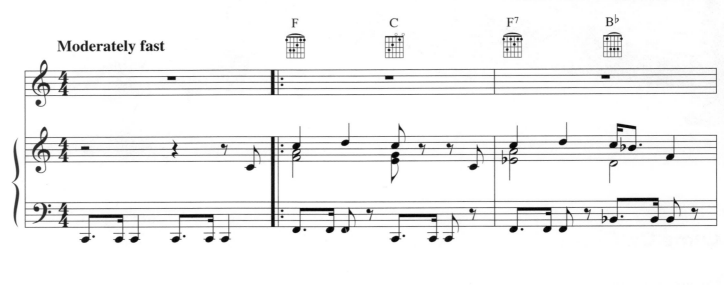

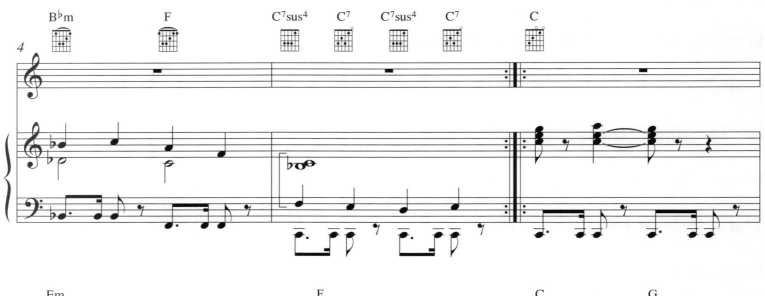

# Dancing Queen

Backing

Words and Music by Benny Andersson,
Bjoern Ulvaeus and Stig Anderson

# Groove Is In The Heart

Words and Music by Kier Kirby,
Dmitry Brill, Towa Tei,
Q-Tip and Herbie Hancock

16

Groove is in the heart.

Groove is in the heart.

Groove is in the heart.

Backing

# Holiday

Words and Music by
Lisa Stevens and Curtis Hudson

# House Of Fun

Backing

Words and Music by
Michael Barson and Lee Thompson

1. Good morn-ing Miss. Can I
(2.) no no Miss, you mis -

3. Party hats, simple enough clear.
   Comprehende savvy understand do you hear?
   A pack of party hats with the coloured tips
   I'm too late Gorgon's heard gossip.
   Well hello Joe, hello Miss Clay many
   Happy returns from the day.

Backing

# The Loco-Motion

Words and Music by
Gerry Goffin and Carole King

**Moderately**

Capo 3

Ev-'ry-bo-dy's do-in' a brand new dance now, c'-mon ba-by, do___ the Lo-co-mo-tion. I know you'll get to like it if you

# Hi Ho Silver Lining

Backing

Words and Music by
Scott English and Laurence Weiss

# Love Shack

Backing

Words and Music by
Catherine Pierson, Frederick Schneider,
Keith Strickland and Cynthia Wilson

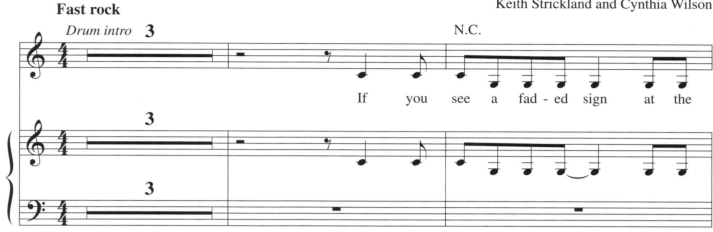

# Walking On Sunshine

Words and Music by Kimberley Rew

# Stayin' Alive

Backing

**Medium rock beat**

Words and Music by Barry Gibb,
Maurice Gibb and Robin Gibb

Well, you can tell

# YOU'RE THE VOICE

**8861A PV/CD**

Casta Diva from Norma - Vissi D'arte from Tosca - Un Bel Di Vedremo from Madam Butterfly - Addio, Del Passato from La Traviata - J'ai Perdu Mon Eurydice from Orphee Et Eurydice - Les Tringles Des Sistres Tintaient from Carmen - Porgi Amor from Le Nozze Di Figaro - Ave Maria from Otello

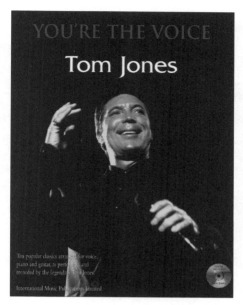

**8860A PVG/CD**

Delilah - Green Green Grass Of Home - Help Yourself - I'll Never Fall In Love Again - It's Not Unusual - Mama Told Me Not To Come - Sexbomb  Thunderball - What's New Pussycat  - You Can Leave Your Hat On

**9297A PVG/CD**

Beauty And The Beast - Because You Loved Me - Falling Into You - The First Time Ever I Saw Your Face - It's All Coming Back To Me Now - Misled - My Heart Will Go On - The Power Of Love - Think Twice - When I Fall In Love

**9349A PVG/CD**

Chain Of Fools - A Deeper Love Do Right Woman, Do Right Man - I Knew You Were Waiting (For Me) - I Never Loved A Man (The Way I Loved You) I Say A Little Prayer - Respect - Think Who's Zooming Who - (You Make Me Feel Like) A Natural Woman

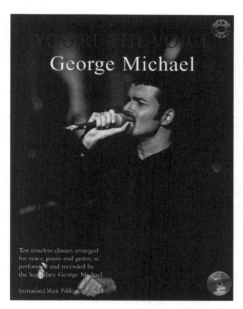

**9007A PVG/CD**

Careless Whisper - A Different Corner Faith - Father Figure - Freedom '90 I'm Your Man - I Knew You Were Waiting (For Me) - Jesus To A Child Older - Outside

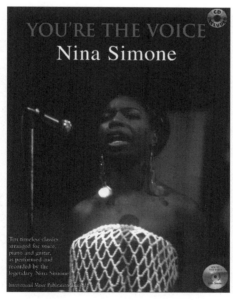

**9606A PVG/CD**

Don't Let Me Be Misunderstood - Feeling Good - I Loves You Porgy  - I Put A Spell On You - Love Me Or Leave Me - Mood Indigo  - My Baby Just Cares For Me Ne Me Quitte Pas (If You Go Away) - Nobody Knows You When You're Down And Out - Take Me To The Water

## The outstanding new vocal series from IMP

### CD contains full backings for each song,
### professionally arranged to recreate the sounds of the original recording

# all woman

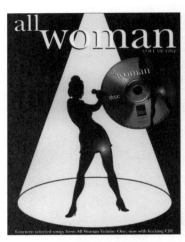

**ALL WOMAN**
**VOLUME 1 PVG/CD 7077A**

All Woman - Cabaret - Can't Stay Away
From You - Eternal Flame - Ev'ry Time We
Say Goodbye - Get Here - I Am What I Am
I Only Want To Be With You - Miss You
Like Crazy - Nobody Does It Better
The Rose - Summertime - Superwoman
What's Love Got To Do With It

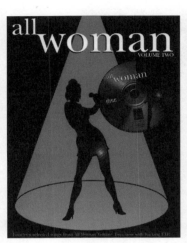

**ALL WOMAN**
**VOLUME 2 PVG/CD 7268A**

Anytime You Need A Friend
Don't It Make My Brown Eyes Blue
Flashdance....What A Feeling - I'll Stand
By You - Killing Me Softly With His Song
One Moment In Time - Pearl's A Singer
(They Long To Be) Close To You - Think
True Blue - Walk On By - The Wind
Beneath My Wings - You Don't Have To
Say You Love Me - 1-2-3

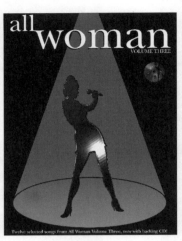

**ALL WOMAN**
**VOLUME 3 PVG/CD 9187A**

Almaz - Big Spender - Crazy For You
Fame - From A Distance - My Baby Just
Cares For Me - My Funny Valentine
The Power Of Love - Promise Me
Respect - Take My Breath Away
Total Eclipse Of The Heart

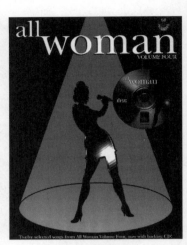

**ALL WOMAN**
**VOLUME 4 PVG/CD 9255A**

Baby Love - Diamonds Are Forever -
Evergreen - For Your Eyes Only - I Will
Survive - If I Could Turn Back Time - I'll
Be There - Rainy Night In Georgia - Send
In The Clowns - Smooth Operator - Sweet
Love - Touch Me In The Morning

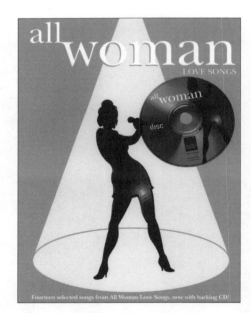

**ALL WOMAN**
**LOVE SONGS PVG/CD 7502A**

All At Once – Anything For You –
Because You Love Me – Crazy For You –
Didn't We Almost Have It All – The
Greatest Love Of All – Here We Are –
Hero – How Do I Live – I'll Never Love
This Way Again – Saving All My Love For
You – Think Twice – The Wind Beneath
My Wings – Without You

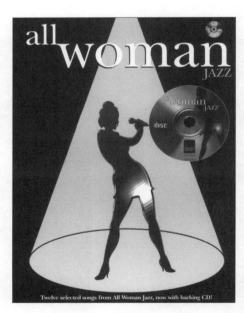

**ALL WOMAN**
**JAZZ PVG/CD 9500A**

Bewitched – Dream A Little Dream Of Me
A Foggy Day – The Girl From Ipanema
I'm In The Mood For Love – In The
Mood – It Don't Mean A Thing (If It Ain't
Got That Swing) – Misty
Nice Work If You Can Get It – On Green
Dolphin Street – 'Round Midnight
Where Or When

## Available from all good music shops